Things Have Disappeared

Things Have Disappeared

Poems by

Sharon Rose-Kourous

© 2024 Sharon Rose-Kourous. All rights reserved.
This material may not be reproduced in any form, published,
reprinted, recorded, performed, broadcast,
rewritten, or redistributed without
the explicit permission of Sharon Rose-Kourous.
All such actions are strictly prohibited by law.

Cover design by Shay Culligan
Cover photo by Helen Kourous
Author photo by Helen Kourous

ISBN: 978-1-63980-582-2

Kelsay Books
502 South 1040 East, A-119
American Fork, Utah 84003
Kelsaybooks.com

For my parents, Betty and Alfred Rose, who taught me everything;
and my children, Helen and George, who taught me the rest;
and grandchildren, Sofia, Liz, and Nikos,
who are teaching me there is more.

Acknowledgments

Thank you to the following publications, in which versions of these poems previously appeared:

Able Muse: "About Time," "Books"
American Poets and Poetry: "Of Spring," "Lake Michigan," "Snow"
Atlanta Review: "A Somehow Lilac"
Blue Unicorn: "Alchemy," "Back Porch," "December," "Deep "Rain," "Nodding Off"
Deeply Shallow: "Afterward"
Disquieting Muses: "Old Maps"
Eclectica: "Reflection"
Edge City: "Dun Aonghasa"
The Formalist: "Duplicity," "Down Reynolds Road," "Orpheus," "Necessity"
Gaia: "Each Leaf Individual"
Lyric: "My Father Was a Carpenter"
Magma: "Consider How the Many-Millioned," "Snowfall," "Exequies," "New Moon," "Voyage"
Melic Review: "Sestina: American Winter," "Keeping God Busy," "After-life"
Octavo: "a.m.," "A Prayer for My Mother"
The Paumanok Review: "Conversation with Strangers"
Pig Iron Press: "My Father Was a Carpenter"
The Piedmont Review: "Still-Life with River," "Eurydice," "Perspective"
Potpourri: "Deceivers," "Snow Angels," "Of Hawks"
The Roanoke Review: "Photographs"
The Rockford Review: "Self Portrait"
Susquehanna Review: "Forecast," "Sonnet for the Longest Night," "Design," "Prodigal Light," "Getting By"
Sparrow: "A Somehow Lilac," "Bluejay"

Contents

A Somehow Lilac	13
Self Portrait	14
Of Spring	15
Productions of Time	16
Alchemy	17
Deceivers	18
Consider How the Many-Millioned	19
December	20
Sestina: American Winter	21
Forecast	23
When the Matter's Done	24
Sonnet for the Longest Night	25
Nodding Off	26
Snowfall	27
(Silence)	28
Windwhirl	29
Design	30
Conversation with Strangers	31
My Father Was a Carpenter	32
Thaw	34
Reflection	35
Still-Life with River	36
Orpheus	37
Visiting Hour	38
Bluejay	39
Willow	40
Keeping God Busy	41
Necessity	42
Asleep in the Past Perfect Tense	43
Lake Michigan, Petosky Stones	44
Exequies	45
Picnic	46
Prodigal Light	47

About Time	48
Afterlife	50
Deep Rain	51
Old Maps	52
New Moon	53
Light. Water	54
Green	55
Back Porch	56
Among the Flowers	57
The Light Broke into Rainbows	58
Each Leaf Individual	59
February Dawn	60
Preparing	61
Snow	62
A Prayer for My Mother	63
Leaving	64
To Be	65
Eurydice	66
The Discovery Channel	67
Twelfth Night	68
Getting By (three sonnets for a passing comet)	69
Implicit in the Blossom	71
Angels	72
Books	73
Burying the Dog	74
Voyage	75
Photographs	76
Along the Shore the Edge Is Altered	77
Dun Aonghasa	78
Snow Angels	79
Perspective	80
Ariel	81
Down Reynolds Road	82
Of Hawks	83

A Somehow Lilac

I keep thinking a somehow lilac
drooping from the green shrub will, although
inside walls, mean spring; that a frolic
of sparrows, roofed, even on antennas, will flow

to hawk-hover above riverglint on outward up-
draft of sudden unshackling. I keep
somehow hoping ice will unstop
and streams, even small ditches will, like deep

tides, moon-stretched, mean something. I even
in lilac evenings see the ghosts of stars.
I remember rivers below birdwing and a child's heaven
wide as night, and constellations of flowers;

we hid below bloomweight; we once were innocent
under walls of lilac; branches down-deep, bent.

Self Portrait

Silly old stick of a woman, muttering she stalks
the lilac paths below the blinking moon;
feet planted firmly one by one. Derisive barks
of dogs follow her; she hums a tuneless tune

and plashes in the puddles, reaches, picks
a rainwet stem of lilac from the neighbor's yard,
and mutters homeward. Moonlight, lonely, licks
across her tousled hair; houselights, barred

and hostile fall along the lawns. Her fingers
fumble in her pockets for the key
that she is always losing; she wonders
if, in other kind of light, perhaps, there'd be

some other kind of vision; someone there before,
who waits her step and opens wide the door.

Of Spring

In the absurd acceptance of the slow uncurl
of leaf (like small hand, trustingly) sun-unfold
-ing tease of spring (unseen spin; my world

on axis flings me skyward) like love hurled
against those splintered stars, I hold
my opening palm to memories of his (leaf,

heart, eyes, sun, stars) held hand. (Reach
into spring and pull the blossom out of bud.) Turn
of earth below such ever-stars, those splattered bright

voices (sighing light and infinite;) absurd,
a cool across my eyes. (Can tears slip
off the edge of earth?) If light were word

(as once they say it was,) can sorrows keep
a silent orbit of their own? Like leaf unfurled
accepts slow sun: I, (alone in) this lonesome world.

Productions of Time

Eternity is in Love with the Productions of Time
—William Blake

What the rock seeks to know, the river
has already transcribed; its fluid
message flashed skyward, its deeper
secrets etched in sand, as though the good

were best ground down to fine and finer siftings
kept hidden beneath slow stone.
What mankind made are finite giftings
fallen along the shore. All else gone,

our one world awakes itself in each new cell
still dividing silently. Rune of wood-grain;
child-mirror of parents' faces, the green well
holding moonlight to a zero: the same

still sift of water past our crumbling shores
while this blue globe fails. Eternity endures.

Alchemy

What everyone says about the hummingbird is O
how their swift wings—! But what I want
is that backward up-and-down flash going
as quickly as light; evening sun slant

rhyming with leaves in the flowerbud air
and the tiltmost high tree branches blazing
before horizon's cutoff; that second when-where
earth's ponderous spin stops and this amazing

instant at the feeder flurries the still
light, silkens nectared air. How he darts
into time and then disappears. What steals
the show is the swift smallness. It parts

the day into itself, as when small rain knows
the alchemy of light and arcs wide rainbows.

Deceivers

The nature of angels, the will of rivers:
both deceive and are intemperate.
No stones may stand where sunlight shivers
on sweet deceitful ripple, though desperate

posturings may hold for some slow time.
What works time's will, works dangers too;
works difficult miracles to my slow mind
that mourns uprooted trees split through,

and wrenched to shore. So those I love
grow old, and sad erosion lines their faces.
Brought nearer now to parting, they leave
sunlit ripples on my memory. I place

a doubter's faith in those old sly deceivers
felling those I love: angels, time, and rivers.

Consider How the Many-Millioned

Consider how the many-millioned sound
of one, each a single flake in free-fall
beyond my two ears, sings one call;
how the million many one flakes downed
beyond my window make one white
for my two eyes which see all one only.
Consider the two-ness of lonely.
In silence and white singing, bright
beyond my one, there is downness of flake-
fall; glide; drift—and each is an all
of other. There is on field and lake
silence simple and white: there is fall-
ing so different from one, as I wake-
ing nightly consider each single flake's call.

December

The trees' great conversation with the sky
comes to a close—a hiatus, rather.
They'll take it up again next summer
when new leaves expect again the old reply

space always gives to earth, always asking why
gravity's clasp pains. "It doesn't matter,"
the void responds. It's the latter's
way of joking about cosmic questions, like the way

light disappears in space. The leafless trees
practice silence now: the stoic's posture;
the still silhouette of the poised dancer
listening for music or envisioning the freeze

at the end of space where time thins out
eternally, leaving to the listener eternal doubt.

Sestina: American Winter

In brittle air the seconds, round as sorrow,
cling shining on the branch; black twigs gleam
and bend, heavy: almost to break; the slow
inexorable build of sleet. Those sad eyes seem
shadow-starred like ice, as stopped time goes
brittle into silence, and slow weight grows

unbearable. And still the burden grows
almost to break. Season of cold sorrow,
early sunset, snow-lost days: last light goes
so quickly; and on her windows gleam
distant other worlds, a universe, it seems,
in traces on the glass where far stars slow

the turning galaxy. She was too chill, too slow
to catch the hour. Though universes grow
in filigree on glass, transformation seems
impossible. When is vapor ice? Does sorrow
arise from joy? What momentary gleam
entrances hope before the instant goes?

Hope fractures in a second, like night-frost goes
suddenly from glass. Rain, sullen, sad and slow
erases a universe. The fragmentary gleam
dies a diamond death. Silence grows
across the galaxies. The stars, like sorrow
all wink out. Why does December seem

so vacant to her now? Midwinter it could seem
the universe stands still as the one star goes
before her yet. This was no winter sorrow.
Hope paced the sky; she followed in her slow
half eager hesitance. How vision grows
before hope halts! So she, toward the gleam,

the vision. But blinded by cold gleam,
the star, the world changed—gone, all that seemed
possible in sky. Now lost. Now swift ice grows
along the wintered stem and now the world goes
stumbling through the galaxy; now hope dies—slow
—or swift—ice builds on branch. Sorrow

weights the world. Sorrow shapes the gleam,
like ice; builds slow, and all things seem
futile. Last hope goes; season's shadow grows.

Forecast

The streets are clabbered with ice and snow
to irritate drivers and send them to ditches
which patiently wait. Simple white. But below,
the old swampland spreads. Time, which is
not a swamp's concern, distantly watches
like a constellation frozen in farther reaches.

And it snows. The sky can't allow
the sun's blank coin with its absent features
to clink into day. Cursing drivers crawl
from tilted car doors: truckers and preachers
resemble each other; their tracks, like stitches
seam the roadside's unraveled edges.

And it snows. As though time desires
this solid appearance; as though it wishes
to stop itself and the world with it,
preserved in this snow this solid ice. The world retires
as a playground for us, but keeps souvenirs:

like a climate-denier, frozen solid, who still sneers.

When the Matter's Done

Where matter and moment intersect,
as at a streetlamp, we collect
inventions of time's collusion with space.
On winter windows, crystals of ice
invert the brilliant sun
and color the floor: it's done
by tricking the watcher's brain
with sleight of light, time and again.

Footprints left in crusted snow
provide eternity with a clue
someone stopped in a moment of time
and made that space, as I this rhyme,
as an act of love, as a moment's applause
for every effect and every cause.

I watch our tracks and know we've been
tracing trails through time again,
where night and wind with silent broom
will sweep us away when the matter's done.

Sonnet for the Longest Night

Increasingly, winters are not intrusion, but the way
the world tilts, habitual; all the clocks
ring an hour later but, still, night's dark
fondles snowslick streets; doe-eyed day
hides at the timid verge. Cold darkness stays
or leaves its footprints. Shadows mock
my venturing-out, while the road to work
grows longer and longer and slick with dismay.

Like a snow statue rigid by its blank front porch
I forget why everything matters. Night is normal,
the stars are not: nothing penetrates cold
though cold's pervasive. Evening, exhaustion. I lurch
from dinner to easy chair to a blanket worn
into my shape—which is shabby, threadbare, increasingly old.

Nodding Off

Peering through the microscope of middle age
at my own puny past: the tricky lens
moves in and out of focus. It all depends
on how the light falls. On the yellowed page
of once-familiar books, there I, no gentle sage
lose half the words; and music simply sends
me nodding off to sleep. The evening ends
all out of focus—and I too old for rage.

No matter now the instrument I choose:
the lenses all are clouded. Random clear
(forgotten) loves float in a mist, and then I lose
a neighbor's face; your photograph, my dear,
detaches from your name. The evening news
though magnified, still tends to disappear.

Snowfall

How snow obscures a landscape is the best
measure of memory messing with time. The crack
and fall of tree reveals a split I'd lost
in old grass, a trail grown shallow, a slack

loss of love. Everything is white, and white
on white, anchored only with spilled scatter of fall;
a litter of empty. Where are we when like late
sparrows in spruce-shelter we scratch through sprawl

of fallen seasons for one rot of nourishment?
It is an old snow, struck at edges with scrape
of plow and black splash of road litter. What I'd meant
was meaning, a trail through new; a bold leap

from mud to light. But winter frosts my window
with icescape, unenterable dimensionless snow.

(Silence)

If she were only *(silence)* still as snow
is; if slow sun like coin of gold hung
(golden); if she were white as cold, as one
blank snowfall-field *(frozen);* if she could go
on petal flakefall silently as white, so
her frozen voice like snowsift whisper flung
about the trees his shadow rests among
—then, silent, frozen, golden, he would know.

Slow sun rides grey above the silent field,
and long cold shadows strike as though time held
motionless as pity; unmoved as winter's weight.
White across the echoed land the cold drifts build
a trackless world. Once and gentle arms *(gold)*
sunflecked *(and silent)* beckon from *(frozen)* white.

Windwhirl

It was a windwhirl bent branches, tossed leaves,
wrestled to earth those stubborn hangers-on
all in one swift moment, so that her maple tree
littered the lawn, covered the grass, laid a blanket down.

Caught in the crannies, swirled by the steps, clogging gutters,
the last leaves let go in a moment, a day, a change in the air:
it's time for the rake, for kids playing in piles; for other
fears and concerns to gather in crannies. A woman's despair

finds no respite when green becomes gold,
when the bare bones of trees stand stern and forthright
accepting the seasons, withstanding the cold,
leaves curled deep in bud, kept hidden from ice.

She refuses the windwhirl, steps onward, hair flying
as stubborn as trees, stern, strong, and defiant.

Design

Inside her yellow room, the long shadow, the broken
light—as though some thousand fireflies
intruded. Evenings, she will waken

and paint the walls with clouds, Ohio skies
and kaleidoscope fields. From her shoulders' ache
she learns fortitude, and paints the thousand ways

prayer is efficacious. Watch: the walls mistake
her brushstrokes' purpose; imagine prophecy
where she intends supplication. Although walls shake

earth holds its course. She smiles and smiles to see
lion and lamb recline in flat Ohio spaces,
and knows her brush designed no simple harmony

but only fireflies whose flickered green replaces
her thousand unspoke prayers, god's thousand faces.

Conversation with Strangers

The moon at least can look at a lake without the slightest
self-pitying refraction. Unlike the conscious
person who, walking the shore, notes the zero is brightest
when growing nearer. He carries the noxious,
not in his pocket, but in those cells he's built of
and the threads which bind them, the guilt of
awareness, the floating zero of which he's the latest

example. His gut distended from Thanksgiving dinner
and conversations with strangers to whom he's related,
he sought the shoreline to walk himself thinner:
committed to healthy living though quite often sated,
he'd like to howl at the moon, but inhibited,
contents himself with the thought he'd exhibited
remarkable constraint with his family's noisiest whiner.

And now there's the moon and himself and the lake
and the moon's faint pull and the pain which of late
multiplies zero in attention-getting pulses
just behind his ribs, which he ignores but knows is
no Thanksgiving guest arriving just after
the table is cleared with belly-filled laughter,
but the stranger he fears; the rilled surface he'll break.

My Father Was a Carpenter

Gentle mythic giant of my childhood astride
the sloping roof, spitting nails precisely
as required by your hammer; your eyes
as blue as love. And I below you hung
precarious, the ladder rungs pressed aching
into the arches of my feet, my world between

earth and rooftop; waiting rescue there between
child and woman, while your silhouette astride
the world blinded me, dark against the aching
heart that hinted only, like the sun, precisely
marking passages. Halfway up the world I hung.
—And you, mysterious, mythic in my eyes.

You'd wipe the sweat and wrinkle up your eyes,
and sing to me, the music caught between
the hammer strokes. Their sharp staccato hung
above the roof-ridge; and I below, astride
some fairytale, handed you the nails precisely
as you needed them. My hands are aching

still, the effort of the height, the fear aching
to be shouted. But no princess in your eyes
could scream from ladder tops. That was precisely
what I could never voice, all my life between
rooftop and earth; and always there astride
the heights and almost falling, I, stubborn, hung

dreaming fairy endings. My childhood hung
above, a castle room, protection from the aching
sun, the blinding sear of light. I stood astride
the world, clinging. Salt stung your eyes
because you could not save me, caught between
pain and pain. But it was this precisely:

I'd handed you the nails. My hand precisely
fed them to your hand. And there we hung
hammered to the sky; no music sang between
your eyes and mine. The bars pressed aching
upward on my feet, sun burned against my eyes.
My father was a carpenter, alone astride

his pain. And I astride my own, precisely
bleeding from the eyes; so we two hung
hammered, nailed, and aching. The heavens held between.

Thaw

Open the window. Allow for a moment the cold
December air to varnish your rooms. Wait
while carpet dust and settled smoke stir up old
dust bunnies in corners. Breathe the white
silk vapor of snow. Discover the mirror
of winter windows behind those blinds: this face
though indistinct is yours. Inside the blur
of grimy glass, your eyes seem haunted, out of place.

Midwinter: Thin daylight hours just balance night
and the ice-sheened moon is horizon's friend.
Accept this rare sun then, this low south light
into your silent year and see: where the river bends
how maple branches seems lace; where even
now buds swell toward spring. The rest is given.

Reflection

There is still that dark window, though lilac fists
unclench hard buds and daffodils
blossom and bend against sharp-edged frost
brittle in the glass. That window still
reflects his face though spring is nearly full
and the sun slips north. Nothing lasts
like a mirror remembering—or a window glass
holding a night's darkness—although sun will
north and north to strike each earlier dawn
against the shutters and migrant birds will follow
starpaths home again, and time creak on
and leaves unfurl to lace the hanging willow

where it brushes the glass with branches green and long
in a pale reflection; although all light is gone.

Still-Life with River

In winter, thinking of flowers where the cold
stream, hung up on dead leaves, goes solid,
she sits, silenced by empty sky, the old
Ohio emptiness. Time and seasons have followed

her here. Hunched in her son's red coat, just
sitting on the backyard swing, she watches
water turn to ice crystal by crystal, crust
first along the shore. Early stars in batches

congenial only to each other appear, sky
seems to want to freeze; everything liquid
wants to stop; everything moving will try
not to, including hope, including her guarded

dreams: this is the age of ice; this still river
forgotten by its source, accepts its crystal cover.

Orpheus

I have been so long a silent passer-by
along such lamplit shadowed ways
where barren branches claw the pallid sky;
where restless moonlight touches, will not stay.

I have grown translucent like the lonesomest
of cloudheld trees: and slender light
passes through me. Aimless as some timelost ghost
I peer in windows, wander in the night

stirred as passing winds will stir the guttered leaf
then wanly drop it back. I cling
to shadows, cloudshapes, shifting shallow grief
fading among the clouds, the darkness echoing

the song I never sing, my voice unheard
whisper of leaves: aimless, dark, windstirred.

Visiting Hour

Locked down to this little room with its nowhere window
overlooking lined asphalt, and fenced-in trees, landscaped
and sickly, probing for earth, for somewhere to grow;
but rooted in chemicals carefully placed
for fast scentless blossoms and excessive green leaves
—shut in this room by his own body's collapse;
tethered by tubes, nutrients, IV's,
all he can watch is the casual cloudscape.

Perhaps it will rain, but he doubts it:
"It's been dry all summer," he says, reduced
to conversational nothings by relatives' shouted
news. His hearing aid's off, his mind seduced
and drugged. Flat on his back, he's grown used to the angle
the sky acquires through his window's rectangle.

Bluejay

It doesn't matter much: a bird, ice-caught,
dead among crumpled ice, its future
gleaming. Glazed on every feather,
a wing in futile reach, not
much more than a blue spill, an after-thought,
a stray song silenced. All day this weather
closed me in. Drowsing by the window,
snow to the sill, I dreamed what cold sky brought.

And it could be my feathered voice, a call
cold as ice-sheen, crystal cloud-gems gathered
each around a grain of doubt: the sudden fall
from dream in sweat-slick fear, the lathered
loss: snow burial, silence, the dark river
and shattered ice. Snow sifting, sifting over.

Willow

(for my father)

A wreck of a willow, rings wrenched, bark torn
digs in at creek-side—its shattered trunk bare.
Naked splintered wood and branches nearly gone
float crazily down the swirling stream—where

a litter of leaves sped first. Stubborn,
stupid, clinging against such floods each year
—and still greening again! Roots against rock turn
and pry, win through, and new-grown stems appear

against all likelihood of life. So you,
toothless, lying in that bed, hopeless against the pain,
naked as a tree and sleeping in your wife's careful arms,
ready to call it quits, beaten, you thought; through—

—were not quite finished. And you, now blossoming again,
stand there beside the stream as spring buds return.

Keeping God Busy

The one moon slants through shutters, sliced
with shadows, and in the dark her cigarette's
a malevolent star; the galaxy's a gnat's
dance ordered by emptiness. What her night's
for: burning in darkness. A toss of dice
contains ordered chaos; and everything gets
the juggler's attention, though he sometimes lets
everything fall in this slatted dark and light.

She could open her shutters, let in stars
to ghost about the room, erase the marks.
But still, the moon's a zero, a reflected gaze
whose random light and shadowed bars
cage the room. Midnight sorrow stays
like a sparrow falling, unnoticed in the dark.

Necessity

How could we have known the harsh necessity
of windows in a shadowed room, half-open
to the heat that shimmers in; how urgency
can lie in shadows by the door, and hope
can step away down hallways, how a voice
retreating down the stairs can slide beneath a door
and lie in humid pools. Given some such choice,
windows pull the sunlight to the floor
where it lies below the drifting sallow smoke
from cigarettes that settles, drifts in layers
of weary lies from faces that have spoken
such lies before. So must windows pull the squares
of light from brilliant canyons of the street
to lie along the floor, expiring in the heat.

Asleep in the Past Perfect Tense

Once she got started with her wet brush, drip-
sided can sitting on an old *New Yorker* to protect
the dust in her carpet; once started, she kept
with that sun-colored paint stroke by stroke, elect-
ing those horizontals at ceiling and baseboard
her private receding terminus, her inward
space-station: everything sun yellow or sky white,—
infinity. She painted even the windowpanes solid
against sunrays whose invisible refraction
insisted against her. She perfected the weight
her brush could carry, the perpendicular stroke
where wall and ceiling meet, the wide sweep
of roller; her rooms became incandescent
as the sun's core.

Litter of work surrounded her: paint cans crusted,
plastic sheeting adhered to the sofa,
the dripped-upon chair accepted splatters
into its varnish, the stepladder sprouted
roots, grew into the carpet; her yellow room blazed
wordlessly. The past perfect tense of a dead
language invented new lyrics in the radio's bleared
voice. From her right index finger pearled
a small red disagreement with the yellow decor.
She curled in fetal position, and slept on the floor.

Lake Michigan, Petosky Stones

Just getting by, you collect fossils and stones
whose mystery's hidden—seen only when wet
in clear ripples, just deep enough to set
your cold legs shivering. Standing up straight, you groan
as your back reminds you your age. Your hair's gotten thin,
and gravity's winning the unfriendly bet
your waistline made. Sanded, you set
your collection high on the beach, admire them;

then toss them all back. Across the long waves,
the sun doubles, then disappears: cold sky
collects colored light, then tumbles it down
beyond the world's rim. Nothing brilliant stays.
On the lorn shore, still just getting by,
you gather your dust for the long ride home.

Exequies

As the dust in the corner escapes once again
the broom, it enjoys a good laugh; at night
it watches the spider and smugly grins:
it's been there. Consider horizons—a sight
grown distantly familiar. Notably absent:
yourself. Remember a cause of the crimson
dalliance of sunset is, after all, dust.

Beneath the floorboards of opulent rooms
circa late 20th C, the scuttling bug
never ponders ontology. Whatever small glooms
are his, the future's not one. Nor the tug
of any emotion not hormonal. Consider love's
utility. Prefer short perspectives over long.
Take survival. Flame your horizon with crimsons.

Picnic

October doesn't whimper
as she puts summer by;

she dresses up in scarlet,
ignores the frowning sky,

and prodigal of apples,
spendthrift of golden coin,

she picnics in the moonlight,
leaving litter on the lawn.

She flings away her garlands,
strips off her summer gown,

and dances in the westwind,
and then—one day—she's gone.

Prodigal Light

From streetlamps she learns to understand
perspective as a property of light. How lone
the evening sidewalks are!—and how restrained
the drawn curtains of her house. As if she'd gone
years ago. Against her wall an evening primrose gleamed
but wrapped itself into a fist with every dawn.

Now nightwind redirects the attitude of leaves.
She slips on running shoes, wants to find the flat
earth and color's absence. Paper houses line the streets,
and branches silhouette like playtoys cut
in some two-dimensioned other life. Only moon's pale
prodigal light is hers. Dry gutters' dark debris
accepts the small stir of her passing, and the low
shadow of her self pulls along behind, grows, retreats.

About Time

Time's efforts at acquiring surface or
entering the stasis of matter, erupt now and then
and graze the sky in steeple, rectangular
clock tower, skyscraper, or pillared Parthenon.
And with a wry twist of cosmic comic perspective,
these acquisitions of earth's museum arrive
at a point (time's antithesis) where collective
layers of carbon residue manage a slime
which destroys 'em. The layered coal
where time first knew itself, those shoals
of seasons, wanted out from the bowels
of dark lack; exchanged heat for the whole
shebang. The industrial ages arrived: revolution.
And filled the air with time's ultimate solution.

These steeples are the quarry's opposite,
and snag bits of sky as though rectangular
were mankind's best habitat
in which to understand himself or capture
a bit of time in which to hide
—or pray, and come at last to perhaps prefer
the liquid light of lakes. Outside,
the tall cathedral's gone green, unsure
of distinctions; and green moss hides
the box that man built as a cure
for lonesomeness. But water glides
and smooths the quarry's severed sides.

Man, busy at his monuments in stone,
invented the quarry, cathedral's opposite,
where light, unstained, filters through the long
liquid aisles where fishes wait
in silver innocence. The carved block rises
against the patient sky: rectangularity
lifts up from the curved uncarved valley
as though to angle cloudshapes from the skies.
These old cathedral towns nestled in the folds
of older hills announce an older desire
—while the serene fish avoiding the lure,
knows nothing of time save generation; holds
to the deep place. And on cathedral spires
collects the residue from which mankind aspires.

Afterlife

The morning mirror forgets your face
and rooms relax their rigorous hold
on things you've kept; the cold
floorboards are space
where dust accumulates.

Everything settles. Still rooms
close inward; windows no longer
accept light. Shadows from corners
fill the floor; evening blooms
as silent as stone.

You're free now. The empty mirror
makes no demands; the walls'
empty rectangles vaguely recall
a still-life there,
reflected, then disappeared.

Deep Rain

Through all the steady night it enters dreams
intent on sleep; drumming on shingles, rushing through eves,
until we dream of oceans and feel moon-pull
hoist us shoreward. This resoundful
rain flattens our faces; sleeping, we sail
to the very edge of silence, its pale
danger brilliant along surfaces. Nearby trees
bend over rooftops, the laden leaves
solicitous above us: sleeping innocent
adventurers—while the unknown continent
cuts the horizon. Slack in each others' arms
we float like pale corpses: one turns,
the other drifts away. Time falls like deep
rain, and takes us as we sleep.

Old Maps

If I'd been better at math perhaps these scrawls
would resemble geometry. A right triangle
could obviate the unflinching parallels
of this city map. My blue Mazda trying to untangle
on ramp from off could also visit our unfinished past
and crumple the zeros—they litter the road, this highway
where all lights are timed to *stop* just
as I accelerate. The laws of inertia
enforce this claim: I'm glad I knew you.
I'm glad we once steamed windows, tangled
sheets; while on clocks, numbers came unglued
and fell to the floor. I'm glad for memory's angled
interruptions, for the ways bodies intersect.
Although the map is faded, my memory's exact.

New Moon

It holds beyondness of bleak. In the perhaps other,
drained. The moon: a solid in sky round
emptiness, it holds the words. Perhaps smothers
them. Silence goes there. Possibly music hounds
your memory chained there. Trees' long black tines
tear at some stars. Clouds, wind-raced, fly; cold
silence finds rootveins' tendrils; lank skeins
unwind in my wrists. Dark. Wonder what holds
the together of me now there is no—
Oh it's a grave thing, this solid silence, this still
windsped moon. See. How my two feet go
waterlapped in twicedark sky, how I will

reflect no light, how the beyond will claim
my lightless after-flight, having no name.

Light. Water

It eluded her for years as she searched that particular
green light-through-leaves that April gives through rain,
receding. Beyond her window always were
bird voice and murmur of water as from a stream
deep-dug in limestone. She wanted that one voice
like a blue jay's sudden cry from deep inside the tall spruce
that hides its inner rot with spiked blue, reaching
always outward. She wanted to know the ways
one can survive the world unsorrowed. The high sun
became her enemy and shadows were her home,
and paler moonlight; she frantic like one
lost in nightmare dream. She walks always alone
through rain and leaf-fall. Moon gleam thrusts its knife
deep in rippled waters. Like a sunken stone, her life.

Green

What wing aloft or leaf unloosed, or flame
afire, ablaze, or out-of-sunset-drawn
jet-thread tugged taut; what flashfire came
like leaf-light? How has green gone
so sudden uncaught; struck from sky-sweep tree
as I was reaching, climbing, clambering to hold
abundant brilliance: leaf on leaf on leaf? Unwary me
to weary and to not watch, not catch the moment gold
grew out of green, caught fire and burned;

failed to loop the scarlet thread unraveling sky;
to tie, twist, take hold and knot that light turned
loose in sky there high, to fling, spin, stray
afire, ablaze. October wing-wind tossed
beyond me careless, heedless, wintered, lost.

Back Porch

The backyard winks from shade to this clear
brilliance as cumulus drift across the sun,
and we in our lazy chairs, mostly silent, stir,
shift our weight, watch the evening's long

casual drift away from day. Our conversation's old,
familiar; lies like a dreaming dog
against our ankles. Everything's been told
and told again. The words are nothing and fall

among the shadows. It's body-comfort, nothing more,
this easy presence, this gathering-in. So near
the danger was, and the one worn chair
so nearly empty. It is enough to hear

each others' voices, while gathered light
sharp along the lawn resists the night.

Among the Flowers

Kneeling among voices of flowers, I add
my own timid song. This soft refrain,
my mother hummed; it was her glad
fingers among the roots, was what she sang

not knowing I could hear. It was her way
of leaving chores and children, to grow
some less contentious things; her day
too filled with household tasks, she'd go

skimming through the door and sing among the flowers,
their music lavender and gold, the green
of leaf.—Her secret song is only hers:
I have long forgot the words. But now I lean

among the colors; her voice is distant, clear;
as I, among the flowers, join the choir.

The Light Broke into Rainbows

Things have disappeared. Although I search
in musty cardboard boxes, on closet shelves,
and corners of the garage, things I loved lurk
only in memory. And they, themselves,

bob to surface unpredictably: for years
I forgot the crystal vase, the wooden bowl,
as though they'd never been. Did they just wear
out and fall to dust? Did children haul

them to the sandbox, leave them in the yard?
Did I ever rub the bowl, touch the grain,
polish the crystal; love the way the light
broke into rainbows, curved along the wood?

—And if I found it now, would I just lose again
your smile my hands caressed by day and night?

Each Leaf Individual

Each leaf individual and lone and each
and every several shining leaf filled,
fed first before it flung beyond all reach
or all returning. Each leaf milled,

swilled all summer long, feasted scarlet light
now lilting earthward; held such sweet gold
along its veins—stored still and April nights
all tender-green. And each leaf individual holds

a summerful, a radiant array; where woods become
bold with that rich light. No easy miracle:
these tall saints lean into amazing flame
and cast their colors down, and each one will

accept the flash
                where fire subsumes
                            all colors into ash
                                          each leaf, each leaf alone.

February Dawn

What trees accomplish: black tangle between
blue and blue, in predawn sky and snow
still layered with night, is a skein

tossed wide as some lithe fishers do
across a wrinkled seaskin. They net some stars
deep-hovering in space, let some slip through

and cast their nets again. This is the still,
the frozen moment—the athlete paused before
the arm flings, the foot rises; this is dawn-dark chill

clarity before her day begins. There are
no other walkers here; neighbors' houses dream
till fumbling hands slam shrill alarms.

Now those sleepers lie still, while stars seek deeper seas
and far-flung nets transform back into trees.

Preparing

I went otherwhere this autumn, otherwhen;
while maples gathered gold, and overhead
the silent hawk stood in sky, I began
a brown leaving. The oak grew red,

and last late bloom of Queen Anne's Lace
frothed beside the road. I took time,
grown loose from stem, time to pace
the leafblack paths. As flocked geese climb

laboring in air, I struggled toward a long release.
Expecting talons, I cleared the clutter, stood
watching the river gather fallen leaves,
swirl them toward the lake: the empty wood

ready for winter, the hawkstruck sky
and otherwhere in autumn, time-freed, I—

Snow

See how the snow erases a summer's work
and blots out autumn's litter—the place
needed a cover-up. The hollyhock,
a skeleton; the Queen Anne's Lace,

ugly a day ago, they now with gossamer grace
make small cathedrals or transitory prayers
worked out in white. Black tree limbs trace
a strong and steady nest for evening stars.

See how the snow obliterates the hours
beyond all memory. See at the window, me:
snowdazzled, warm, and heedless of the years
freezing into ice. In frost-built reverie

my small ice castles rise: dreams can sometimes drift
across the brittle broken litter of the past.

A Prayer for My Mother

Where she walks punching the ground with her cane,
may the earth lie without humps or hollows,
that her brittleness reach the backyard swing,
that her careful step, as each slow foot follows
the other, reach this simple destination;
that she may in the maple tree's shade
name the day's birds; that finches station
themselves nearby and sing for her, unafraid.
May I, tense behind the window curtain
not rush out to help her; may she arrive,
stubborn and solid wherever she's going;
may birds be there, instead of angels, singing;

may she leave from level ground, without my knowing;
her cane propped in a corner, unneeded for winging.

Leaving

One spring morning the maple remembered:
Leaves! My father, forgetting yesterday,
knows exactly what groceries he delivered
to whom fifty years ago. I watch the way

he travels time; selects the memory
which fits his moment's needs. Autumn-umbered,
the trees will lose summer's green and stark weight
of ice will winter empty branches. Then, feathered

with April, they will summer well, unbothered
by icy recollections. My father will stay
silent by the window, held by the gathered
clear-as-ice; the brilliant long-gone days,

turn them in his hands; and while I grieve
in April's cruel light, he remembers. *Leaves.*

To Be

> "To be *is* to be perceived."
> —George Berkeley

The thing is, you're not allowed a lilac
now and then. Evenings always hasten
down the west, stumbling like an alcoholic
fumbling and anxious for the hidden

respite. Your car prefers the driveway
to the garage; you, your briefcase
full of papers to take back the other way
tomorrow. Your paycheck's no relief, stays

an electronic blip, error message flashing;
and your family's sleepily ensconced
by the TV screen. Round red sun, crashing
into fragile night, stumbles, vomits once—

then goes to guttered sleep. Though it deserved
more, the garden's vanished. Unobserved.

Eurydice

(men can't follow directions!)

"Like, he was my boy-toy; I his squeeze,"
(and, oh! the music that they made
laughing in fields, dancing the glade—
A tragic snake-bite on her knees;
an allergic reaction, swift chills and a sneeze,)
*"And before we knew it, I was, like, dead
and laid to rest in a hard cold bed,
and I was, like, captured in dark Hades."*

(He followed her there; and brought his lyre;
he sang, and the gods forgot to glower
and she followed him out of that darksome bower.)
"Like, we nearly escaped! Like, all was well!"

(But—it's the nature of men, sadly I tell,)
"He couldn't do directions; and I'm, like, stuck in hell."

The Discovery Channel

This light-dance arriving from the edge of time
a choreograph of ultimate and wonderful
becomings; a rainbow on my tv screen
like some vague Disney production, squander-ful
of marvels between the ads; it pins this small
star-stuff self against that eons-empty place
where galaxies spin outward; and all
my pitiful attempts at meaning seem to race
outward in emptiness. That Webb-visioned space
spins also here inside, and I dare not consider
dust contemplating dust and sitting here amazed:
star-sharing-self; a nano-second wonder

consuming the munchies the ads extol
and grasping the remote, but losing control.

Twelfth Night

Up to their flat eyes in snow, opaque
smiles, round mouths caroling no song,

a forgotten plywood choir still waits
the miracle which put them there, strung

with glitter-lights. Surprise
O's their lips—this snow burial's a thing

they never dreamed. Their two-dimensioned eyes
peer across the drifts. What should they sing,

what wonder now proclaim? Unprepared
by their warm attic past, how could they know

this depth, this cold, this darkness where
new storms arrive to bury plywood miracles?

Getting By (three sonnets for a passing comet)

I

If you require a mirror, much-wished-upon stars
quit that job within my generation;
they twinkle, twinkle where they are,
distracted from you by odd constellations
that came after Sputnik: the nearer reaches are junky
with orbiting dreams. Don't look at skies
for fixed points; don't decide based on clunky
reflections from space-flotsam whose orbit defies
our old friend, gravity. Peer into lakes
instead. Through clear waters, old stones
ripple near your toes; your moving face
recedes: fossils, old as stars, hone
   their edges for you. Then should you peer
   past surface-shift: see—your probable future.

II

If you require a mirror, avoid love;
its inward gaze fails to reflect,
absorbs all lengths of light. Try to leave
the old neighborhood; become a derelict,
a wanderer. Exile isn't always an end,
but a means, as Odysseus found after detour
and divertissement; and travels lend
you an air of purpose you'd lacked before:
that's why glass held such attraction
in your youth. You needed a place for time
to settle in. Now, mapped, your face's subtraction
from the environment allows light's pure line
   the comfort of shadow in distances where
   if you look through love's glass, you might reappear.

III

If you require a mirror, look to surfaces,
where you will find, reversed, that dim
smile, surprising in its vague disturbances
of terrain you've come to think of as your own.
Do this over time, get used to change
in those reflected shifts of light; the cold
straight-line lessons of years. Begin to arrange
your features toward gravity; begin to hold
heavy things more lightly; prepare to lose
surfaces into which you peered; try to convey
an aura of bumbling confidence. Or choose
eccentricity. Just after sunset, pray
   that a comet blinking through an April sky
   reflects you, for a moment, just getting by.

Implicit in the Blossom

Implicit in the blossom, the bud's long wait
green below the bark, implicit in the mirror,
the years of silence. Easy to forget
during the slow drift of pollen, how failure
is far more frequent; how ice can break
even the supple bough; how roots can die
easily and without protest, how glass can wait
emptier than stars battered against the sky.

I wander through these foolish empty rooms
sweeping echoes from the silent floor;
wipe anger from the corners, take down the mirror.
Implicit in the bud as in the bloom
is season's end, the turned key and locked door:
implicit in the falling leaf, the autumn fire.

Angels

They are. In the moment of fracture
where atoms split or sear; where winter takes
still ice from liquid silver edge of lake;
or light becomes a rainbow. The capture
of angels involves violence and rapture,
and changes instantly. The sinister brilliant shake
of raptor-feather, flight-bound; the brim-break
of tears through lashes; the limb-loose laughter
of children playing: they are the suddenly here
angels; they rise and rise, sprung of
sharp inversions. They soar and sear
in tree-twist wind; they only love
the swift instant, the cold split, the near
benison of bells; the way things weave.

Books

   (for C. E.)

I still have some of your books, safely kept,
though dusty, stacked high beside the window
on a shelf. The couch where you slept
lost its impression of you, although

some sort of aftershave lingered, a scent
rather unlike you. The books slip
when trucks rattle the house, but can't
decide to fall. It's the way of things I keep

but don't own. As though entropy
can be fought, as if a layer of dust will preserve
a friend's smile, and time's touch will be
milder than street-rattle; perhaps will swerve

away from here—or perhaps friends return to claim
these worn left-behinds, waiting like souvenirs
reversed. Some things stay the same
though all things change. Your books are here.

Burying the Dog

Swearing and crying you wiped eyes and nose
on the rough sleeve of your red coat
behind the garage where blue spruce throw
dark needles against the frosted ground.

Your spade grinding rock in your stubborn
refusal to find a more amenable grave,
you shoveled, hollered, cursed, until worn
past your sorrow you gave

one last smoothing to yellow clay's cut.
You sat and smoked half hoping I would see
and scold you for the smoke, hand you a just
reason for anger. Then quieter, bleak,

you buried him in my best blanket, alone
as you had to be, and tramped the dark earth down.

Voyage

Heavy with their mutual sweat, their sheets lie
tumbled like froth at high tide line.
As they ebb into sleep, she watches his eyes
darting behind their lids, and turns to tongue
them; the salt of his skin like the sea
drifts her into buoyant dreams.

They could voyage to the far antipodes
and sleep on salt shores under a foreign sun;
triangulate the stars to find out when
noon bells ring at Greenwich only for curiosity
and not for need of time. Though they might scan
the horizon for sails, no cold necessity
laps their shores. The tidal moon will wake
and rouse their salt-slick bodies as they sleep.

Photographs

Next year's leaves lie so deep inside each stem
there is no guessing if cold slim rays
of winter's wanlight reach them; frost ices them
with brittle light. Survival stays

upon such fragile hopes—and photographs can only feed
a half-day's dream; there is no sustaining
self on these. Fence-lines meet the battered weed,
and cornered leaves catch warmth: remaining

sheltered is surviving when such icy light
cuts along the snow, and the buried memories
hid in fragile twigs are covered deep from sight
by dangerous sleet—and what of bud below?—these

photographs she found, these fragments of forgotten years,
lie in a litter. Ice-burdened, broken, they disappear.

Along the Shore the Edge Is Altered

The willow, top-heavy, hollow, westward bent,
went first in the wind. It lies
by the fast-flowing creek. Where the wind sent
all those leaves is a mystery. The trunk, tried,
twisted, stressed to shaken shape stands white
and torn; the grain where all those years
are kept in circles, splintered now. Late
long October light knifes across, wears
a beneficent evening color now; the wind's rage
wore out this morning. Along the shore
the edge is altered. I knew the lay
of this land gone suddenly unfamiliar
as, coiled below the bark, now westward sent,
the willow knew its secret circled calendar.

Dun Aonghasa

(Inis Mór, Ireland)

Feet find a scrambling way, and every step
is dangerous—the long slow slant, the rocks
in helter-skelter slabs; the narrow way, the slap
of unseen waves on stones below: the mind blocks

and balks, the feet move on. The low sky warns
the wanderer: this is no safe height; this edge
is ultimate. Sheer cliff calls, danger charms
and fascinates. Wind pulls her toward the ledge

where high rock leans above the crashing sea;
and wind presses, pushes, sends her straight
beyond extremity. The wind-whipped mind can be
in such straits, can lean at cliff tops, break

and sigh like sea's white foam, the force
raging at the rocks below, the swift recourse.

Snow Angels

Oh these are deeper angels fallen on the snow
than she expected: black wings spread,
slipping into mud, ice crusting earth below—
sad diamonds that melt to muck instead
of those bright wings, no trumpets' one clear cry
cleaving all the air, no clarion
announcement slicing through the frozen sky
and making all things clear in swift decision.

Some children shaped these fallen frozen forms
then wandered on: their melting tracks meander
fading into slush. The repetitious sun,
though winter-weak will send these angels under,
and earth will slowly turn, and no one know
the brilliant moment shaped—then melted—in the snow.

Perspective

From Hale-Bopp's perspective, this backyard
with me in it just might offer evidence
of matter's curiosity. Though it's heard
the slow silence of time ever since
the first bang's echo died, it's watched
this blue globe carefully, not seeking
affirmation or company, but aware a batch
or a stir or a soup could come sneaking
into the heavenly harmonies. So the glint
of my binoculars here in April could concern
the good of the order, might be a hint
of something changed. Bopp might want to learn
more itself; make a note that it's found
a dangerous spark to observe the next time around.

Ariel

The sky is big tonight, the clouds low;
between them and the green earth, the long
light of sunset slants through rain. I hope
for wind: leaf-ripping, branch-searing lean
of tornado-starter wind, some hard wind
to test how firmly root can cling, to try
the fibrous core; something to resist,
hold desperately against. Rain-lashed, I lay
shoulder and back against rough bark, let my roots grasp,
grow stubborn leaves, reach wind's great play,
and draw it to me.   Each simple day I go
tamely off to mundane tasks, belong
to carpools, flower-funds, kid play-dates—and daily hope
for Fridays.
          But tonight, I'm feeling low, and mean.

Down Reynolds Road

Dreaming down the daily darkened road
the sun an edge of light, an air
brightening and unattainable—the slow
command of stoplights earths me here
on this small arc; this wedge I cut
daily from the great untouched horizon
of all my other dreams, the dawnlight shut
from other lusts, the night's desire gone
to coffee cups and toast, familiar street,
familiar year, familiar round, familiar groan
of my small segment of the universe.

                                        Delete
a single day: the arc collects itself and spins
the swimming earth.

                  The workday still begins.

Of Hawks

Give me the night visitor who tattoos
my wrist and takes me all
in an instant.
                    Give me death that knows
my number as the secret flow
my heartbeats count, that takes me all
completely.
                    Beyond my window now:
feathers and bloodstained snow
memorialize the dove—nothing shows
of hawkstrike.
                    It took all
my strength to watch and know
the dove fortunate. It's slow
diminishment one dreads—and that is all.

About the Author

A lifelong native of NW Ohio and SE Michigan, Sharon Rose-Kourous taught high school literature and language arts, spending most of her career at a suburban public school. A single parent, she finds her poetry arises from lawn-mower fumes and dust-bunnies under the beds; from dirty dishes and unwashed windows; from the parenting moments and the hours spent grading essays; it is tempered by the quiet stubborn, stoic, and repressed ethos of the Midwest family and neighbors who molded her childhood. It is poetry fed on sunsets and cornfields, snow-sifting skies and weeds growing by the wayside. As an escape from teaching and parenting, her poetry may have saved her sanity. It found widespread publication in print and online. *Things Have Disappeared* is her first full-length collection, and will soon be followed by a second, now in the hopper with Cornerstone Press.

www.ingramcontent.com/pod-product-compliance
Lightning Source LLC
Chambersburg PA
CBHW030911170426
43193CB00009BA/814